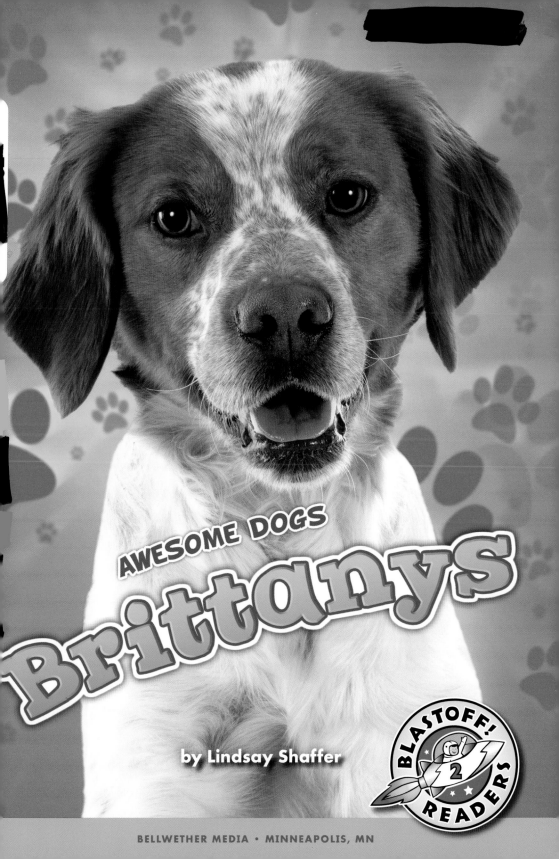

AWESOME DOGS

Brittanys

by Lindsay Shaffer

BLASTOFF! READERS

2

BELLWETHER MEDIA · MINNEAPOLIS, MN

BR 636.752

Note to Librarians, Teachers, and Parents:

Blastoff! Readers are carefully developed by literacy experts and combine standards-based content with developmentally appropriate text.

Level 1 provides the most support through repetition of high-frequency words, light text, predictable sentence patterns, and strong visual support.

Level 2 offers early readers a bit more challenge through varied simple sentences, increased text load, and less repetition of high-frequency words.

Level 3 advances early-fluent readers toward fluency through increased text and concept load, less reliance on visuals, longer sentences, and more literary language.

Level 4 builds reading stamina by providing more text per page, increased use of punctuation, greater variation in sentence patterns, and increasingly challenging vocabulary.

Level 5 encourages children to move from "learning to read" to "reading to learn" by providing even more text, varied writing styles, and less familiar topics.

Whichever book is right for your reader, Blastoff! Readers are the perfect books to build confidence and encourage a love of reading that will last a lifetime!

This edition first published in 2019 by Bellwether Media, Inc.

No part of this publication may be reproduced in whole or in part without written permission of the publisher. For information regarding permission, write to Bellwether Media, Inc., Attention: Permissions Department, 6012 Blue Circle Drive, Minnetonka, MN 55343.

Library of Congress Cataloging-in-Publication Data

Names: Shaffer, Lindsay, author.
Title: Brittanys / by Lindsay Shaffer.
Description: Minneapolis, MN : Bellwether Media, Inc., [2019] | Series:
   Blastoff! Readers. Awesome Dogs | Audience: Age 5-8. | Audience: Grade K
   to 3. | Includes bibliographical references and index.
Identifiers: LCCN 2018031915 (print) | LCCN 2018036179 (ebook) | ISBN
   9781681036380 (ebook) | ISBN 9781626179073 (hardcover : alk. paper)
Subjects: LCSH: Brittany spaniel–Juvenile literature.
Classification: LCC SF429.B78 (ebook) | LCC SF429.B78 S55 2019 (print) | DDC 636.752–dc23
LC record available at https://lccn.loc.gov/2018031915

Editor: Betsy Rathburn   Designer: Laura Sowers

Printed in the United States of America, North Mankato, MN.

Table of Contents

What Are Brittanys?   4

Long Legs and Friendly Faces   6

History of Brittanys   12

Happy Hunters   16

Glossary   22

To Learn More   23

Index   24

What Are Brittanys?

Brittanys are smart, energetic dogs. They love to hunt and play dog sports.

These dogs are **devoted** pets. They love being part of the family.

Brittanys are a medium-sized **breed**. They weigh up to 40 pounds (18 kilograms).

Long legs help these dogs run fast. Their folded ears flap behind them as they run!

Brittanys have soft, friendly faces.
Their noses are brown, pink,
or tan.

Brittany Coats

brown

orange

Most Brittany **coats** are **bi-color**. They may be white with orange or dark brown fur.

Brittany Profile

— floppy ears

thick coat —

— long legs

Life Span: 10 to 14 years

Trainability:

| 1 | 2 | 3 | 4 | 5 | 6 |

Hardest to train   Easiest to train

Brittany coats have different patterns, too. **Piebald** and **roan** are popular patterns.

Brittanys may have straight or wavy fur.

History of Brittanys

Brittanys first came from the Brittany **region** of France. They became popular working dogs in western Europe.

France

N
W E
S

They often worked as hunters
and guard dogs.

Brittanys arrived in the
United States in 1932.

In 1934, they joined the **Sporting Group** of the **American Kennel Club**.

Brittanys love hunting birds!
They find and fetch birds for
human hunters.

Brittanys are a **pointing breed**. When they spot a bird, they point their bodies towards it.

Brittanys are great family pets.
They enjoy playing outside
and hiking.

agility course

Many Brittanys enjoy dog sports such as **agility** and **flyball**.

Brittanys are **loyal** and loving.
These dogs are even friendly
with strangers.

Each day is an adventure
for Brittanys!

Glossary

agility—a dog sport where dogs run through a series of obstacles

American Kennel Club—an organization that keeps track of dog breeds in the United States

bi-color—a coat pattern that has two colors, one being white

breed—a type of dog

coats—the hair or fur covering some animals

devoted—loving

flyball—a relay race for dogs that involves obstacles and retrieving balls

loyal—having constant support for someone

piebald—a coat of white fur with patches of another color

pointing breed—a type of hunting dog that points to birds with its whole body

region—a part of a country

roan—a coat pattern with colored and white hairs mixed together

Sporting Group—a group of dog breeds that are active and need regular exercise

To Learn More

AT THE LIBRARY
Gagne, Tammy. *The Dog Encyclopedia for Kids.* North Mankato, Minn.: Capstone Young Readers, 2017.

Gagne, Tammy. *Spaniels, Retrievers, and Other Sporting Dogs.* North Mankato, Minn.: Capstone Press, 2017.

Sommer, Nathan. *Cocker Spaniels.* Minneapolis, Minn.: Bellwether Media, 2018.

ON THE WEB

FACTSURFER

Factsurfer.com gives you a safe, fun way to find more information.

1. Go to www.factsurfer.com.

2. Enter "Brittanys" into the search box.

3. Click the "Surf" button and select your book cover to see a list of related web sites.

Index

agility, 19

American Kennel Club, 15

birds, 16, 17

breed, 6, 17

coats, 9, 10

color, 8, 9

ears, 7, 10

Europe, 12

faces, 8

family, 5, 18

fetch, 16

flyball, 19

France, 12

fur, 9, 11

guard dogs, 13

hiking, 18

hunt, 4, 13, 16

legs, 7, 10

life span, 10

noses, 8

patterns, 10

pets, 5, 18

play, 4, 18

pointing breed, 17

run, 7

size, 6

Sporting Group, 15

strangers, 20

trainability, 10

United States, 14

The images in this book are reproduced through the courtesy of: cynoclub, front cover; Christian Mueller, p. 4; Eric Isselee, pp. 5, 9 (all); Lesley Elizabeth Adams, p. 6; Marko25, pp. 7, 13; Cristian Umili, pp. 8-9; cynoclub, p. 10; digitalfarmer, p. 11; Emmanuelle Grimaud, p. 12; Tierfotoagentur/ Alamy, p. 14; tbird3077, p. 15; Steve Oehlenschlager, p. 16; mauritius images GmbH/ Alamy, p. 17; GROSSEMY VANESSA/ Alamy, p. 18; Skumer, p. 19; kali9, p. 20; everydoghasastory, p. 21.